Jupiter
The Largest Planet

By Daisy Allyn

Gareth Stevens
Publishing

Please visit our Web site, www.garethstevens.com. For a free color catalog of all our high-quality books, call toll free 1-800-542-2595 or fax 1-877-542-2596.

Library of Congress Cataloging-in-Publication Data

Allyn, Daisy.
Jupiter : the largest planet / Daisy Allyn.
    p. cm. — (Our solar system)
Includes index.
ISBN 978-1-4339-3822-1 (pbk.)
ISBN 978-1-4339-3823-8 (6-pack)
ISBN 978-1-4339-3821-4 (lib. bdg.)
1. Jupiter (Planet)—Juvenile literature. I. Title.
QB661.A45 2010
523.45—dc22
                                    2010003385

First Edition

Published in 2011 by
Gareth Stevens Publishing
111 East 14th Street, Suite 349
New York, NY 10003

Copyright © 2011 Gareth Stevens Publishing

Designer: Daniel Hosek
Editor: Greg Roza

Photo credits: Cover, p. 1, back cover NASA/JPL/Space Science Institute; pp. 5, 7 Shutterstock.com; pp. 9, 19 (Jupiter and moons), 21 Getty Images; p. 11 NASA/ESA; pp. 13 (Jupiter), 19 (Ganymede) NASA/JPL; p. 13 (Earth) © Photodisc; pp. 15, 17 NASA/JPL/University of Arizona.

Printed in the United States of America

CPSIA compliance information: Batch #CS10GS: For further information contact Gareth Stevens, New York, New York at 1-800-542-2595.

Contents

Boldface words appear in the glossary.

Meet the Giant Planet

Jupiter is the fifth planet from the sun. It is the largest planet in the **solar system**. Jupiter is about 11 times wider than Earth!

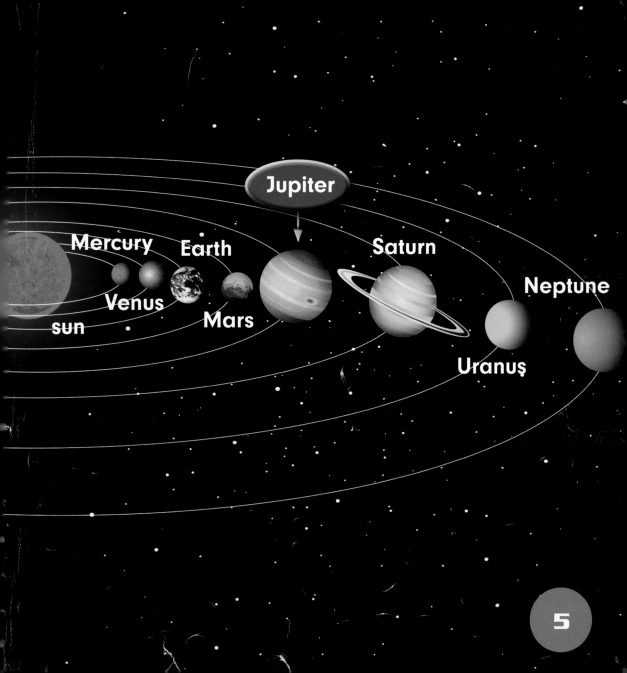

Get Moving

Jupiter **orbits** the sun just like the other planets. Jupiter takes almost 12 years to orbit the sun just once!

sun

Jupiter

7

Jupiter also spins around just like the other planets. Jupiter spins very fast. The planet spins all the way around in less than 10 hours!

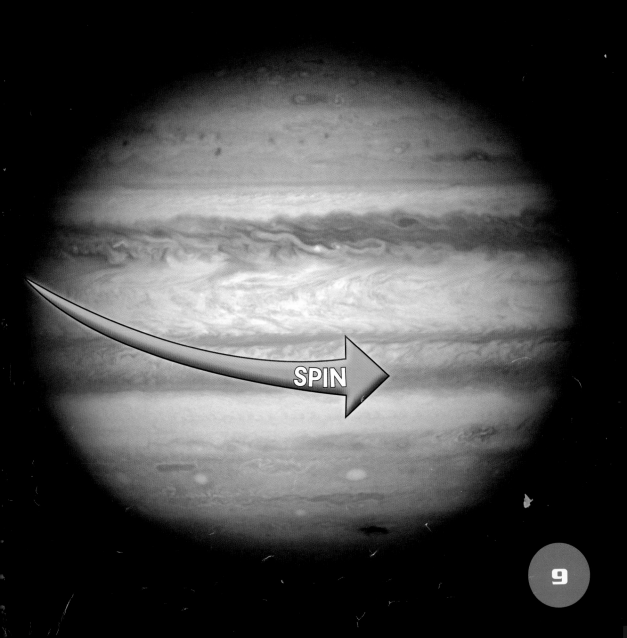

SPIN

9

Where the Wind Blows

Jupiter is covered with clouds. Strong winds blow the clouds in different directions. This is why Jupiter looks like it has stripes.

Jupiter has many storms. The Great Red Spot is the biggest storm in the solar system. It is so big it could swallow Earth!

Great Red Spot

Earth

The Gas Giant

Jupiter is called a "gas giant" because its outer **layer** is made of gases. It does not have solid ground like Earth does. Jupiter's main gases are **hydrogen** and **helium**.

Beneath the gas clouds, Jupiter is made up mostly of liquid hydrogen and liquid helium. Scientists think Jupiter's small center is hot and rocky.

hydrogen and
helium gas

rocky center

liquid hydrogen
and helium

The Moons of Jupiter

Jupiter has more than 60 moons. Jupiter's moon Ganymede (GA-nih-meed) is the biggest moon in the solar system. It is larger than the planet Mercury!

moons of Jupiter

Ganymede

Rings Around Jupiter

In 1979, scientists discovered Saturn is not the only planet with rings. A space **probe** showed that Jupiter has rings, too. They are much harder to see than Saturn's rings.

moon of Jupiter

Jupiter's rings

probe

Glossary

helium: one of the most common gases in the solar system

hydrogen: a common gas. The most common matter in the solar system.

layer: a thickness of something lying under or over another

orbit: to travel in a circle or oval around something

probe: an unmanned spaceship

solar system: the sun and all the space objects that orbit it, including the planets and their moons

For More Information

Books

Loewen, Nancy. *The Largest Planet: Jupiter*. Minneapolis, MN: Picture Window Books, 2008.

Taylor-Butler, Christine. *Jupiter*. New York, NY: Children's Press, 2008.

Web Sites

Jupiter

www.kidsastronomy.com/jupiter.htm

Read interesting facts about Jupiter and see diagrams.

Solar System Exploration: Jupiter

solarsystem.nasa.gov/planets/profile.cfm?Object=Jupiter&Display=Kids

This site from NASA explores Jupiter and its many moons.

Index

About the Author

Daisy Allyn teaches chemistry and physics at a small high school in western New York. A science teacher by day, Allyn spends many nights with her telescope, exploring the solar system. Her Great Dane, Titan, often joins Allyn on her nightly star-gazing missions.